'Drawn on by his eagerness for the open sky, he left his guide and soared upwards . . .'

PUBLIUS OVIDIUS NASO
Born 43 BC, Sulmo, Italy
Died AD 17, in exile

Taken from Books VIII and IX of Mary M. Innes's
translation of *Metamorphoses*.

OVID IN PENGUIN CLASSICS
*The Erotic Poems*
*Fasti*
*Heroides*
*Metamorphoses*

# OVID

## *The Fall of Icarus*

*Translated by*
Mary M. Innes

PENGUIN BOOKS

PENGUIN CLASSICS

Published by the Penguin Group
Penguin Books Ltd, 80 Strand, London WC2R ORL, England
Penguin Group (USA) Inc., 375 Hudson Street, New York, New York 10014, USA
Penguin Group (Canada), 90 Eglinton Avenue East, Suite 700, Toronto, Ontario,
Canada M4P 2Y3 (a division of Pearson Penguin Canada Inc.)
Penguin Ireland, 25 St Stephen's Green, Dublin 2, Ireland
(a division of Penguin Books Ltd)
Penguin Group (Australia), 707 Collins Street, Melbourne, Victoria 3008, Australia
(a division of Pearson Australia Group Pty Ltd)
Penguin Books India Pvt Ltd, 11 Community Centre, Panchsheel Park,
New Delhi – 110 017, India
Penguin Group (NZ), 67 Apollo Drive, Rosedale, Auckland 0632, New Zealand
(a division of Pearson New Zealand Ltd)
Penguin Books (South Africa) (Pty) Ltd, Block D, Rosebank Office Park,
181 Jan Smuts Avenue, Parktown North, Gauteng 2193, South Africa

Penguin Books Ltd, Registered Offices: 80 Strand, London WC2R ORL, England

www.penguin.com

This selection published in Penguin Classics 2015
001

Set in 10/14.5 pt Baskerville 10 Pro
Typeset by Jouve (UK), Milton Keynes
Printed in Great Britain by Clays Ltd, St Ives plc

A CIP catalogue record for this book is available from the British Library

ISBN: 978-0-141-39867-9

www.greenpenguin.co.uk

Penguin Books is committed to a sustainable
future for our business, our readers and our planet.
This book is made from Forest Stewardship
Council™ certified paper.

When the morning star had banished the night, unveiling the brightness of the day, the East wind fell, and rainclouds gathered in the sky. Sped on his way by the mild South wind, Cephalus returned home, accompanied by the sons of Aeacus. After a prosperous voyage they reached the harbour they were making for, sooner than they had dared to hope.

Meanwhile Minos was plundering the shores of Megara, and trying out his military strength against the town of Alcathous, where Nisus ruled. This venerable white-haired king had one bright purple tress right in the middle of his head. On its safety depended the safety of his kingdom.

The rising moon was now displaying her horns for the sixth time, and still the outcome of the struggle hung in the balance. Winged victory had long been hovering between the two sides, undecided. There was a tower belonging to the king, built on to those tuneful city walls where Leto's son, they say, laid down his golden lyre, so that its music was imparted to the masonry. Often in the days of peace Nisus' daughter had been in the habit of climbing up there, and flinging pebbles against the stones to make them ring. During the war, too, she used often to watch the grim struggle from that vantage point and, as the conflict dragged on, she had come to know the names of the leaders and to recognize their arms and their horses, their attire and their Cretan quivers. Better than any of the others, she knew their general, Europa's son; indeed she knew him better than she should have done. In her eyes, Minos was perfect. When he wore his helmet with its plumed crest, she thought how handsome he looked in a helmet; if he was carrying his shield of shining bronze, the shield became him well; when, with straining muscles, he hurled his pliant spear, the princess praised his strength and skill: when he fitted an arrow to his bowstring and bent the bow in a wide arc, she swore that Apollo looked just like that when he stood with his arrows in his hand. But when Minos laid aside his helmet and revealed his features, when, decked in purple, he bestrode his white horse with its embroidered trappings and pulled on its foam-flecked bit, Nisus' daughter was almost driven out of her senses, and was all but out of her mind with love. Happy the javelin he touched, she declared, and happy the reins he gathered in his hands. Had it but been possible, her impulse was to rush to him, braving the enemy's lines, though she was only a girl. She wanted to throw herself from the top of some tower, into the Cretan camp, or to open to the enemy the gates that brazen bolts held fast, or to do anything else to please Minos. As she sat gazing at the shining canvas of the Cretan king's tent, 'I do not know,' she mused, 'whether to be glad or sorry that this miserable war is being fought. I am sorry that Minos is my enemy, when I love him so: but if there had been no war, I should never have known him! Now, if he were to take me as a hostage, he could abandon the war, and have me as his companion, as a pledge of peace. O my handsome hero, if your mother was herself as beautiful as you, it is no wonder that a god fell in love with her! Thrice blessed would I be, if I could take wing and, gliding through the air, light down in the camp of the Cretan king, there to confess my feelings and my love, and ask what dowry would make Minos take me for his wife: anything, short of my father's kingdom! For I would rather lose the marriage I dream of, than obtain it by treachery: though indeed many people have found it profit them to be defeated, when their victor has been reasonable and kindly. There is no doubt that Minos is justified in waging war to avenge his murdered son: he is strong in the cause for which he fights, strong in the arms that defend it. We shall be conquered, I feel sure, and if that is the fate that awaits our city, why should not I, in my love, open up these gates to him, instead of waiting for his military strength to breach the walls? It is better that he should be able to win without delay, without slaughter, without the cost of his own blood. At any rate, I should not then have to fear lest someone unwittingly wound your breast, my Minos. Unwittingly, I say, for there is no one so hard-hearted that he would dare to aim his cruel spear against you, if he knew who you were.'

The plan she had begun to make appealed to her, and she resolved to give herself up to Minos, with her father's kingdom as a dowry, and so put an end to the war. But the will to do this was not enough.

'There is a garrison on sentry duty at the entrance to the city,' she said to herself, 'and my father has the keys to the gates. Wretched girl that I am, he is the only one I have to fear: he alone prevents me from accomplishing what I desire. Would to the gods I were rid of my father! But surely every man is his own god: Fortune refuses her aid to those who merely pray, and take no action. Anyone else, fired with a desire as great as mine, would long ago have destroyed anything that stood in the way of her love, and have been glad to do so. Why should I be less brave than another? I would make my way boldly through fire and sword, and in this case there is no need of either, but only of a lock of my father's hair. That lock is more precious to me than gold, for the purple tress will make me happy, and bring me that for which I pray!' As she was musing thus, night, the mighty healer of men's cares, came on, and with the darkness she grew bolder. During those first peaceful hours, when sleep enfolds the hearts of mortals whom day's anxieties have wearied, she silently entered her father's bedroom, and performed her awful deed. His own daughter robbed her father of the hair on which his whole destiny depended. When she had obtained her horrible prize, she made her way through the very midst of the enemy – so confident was she in the service she had done them – till she came to the king. He was startled by her arrival, but she addressed him in these words: 'Love has driven me to crime. I, Scylla, daughter of King Nisus, hand over to you the gods of my country and my home. I ask nothing in return except yourself. Take this pledge of my love, this purple tress of hair, and believe that it is not my father's hair but his head which I deliver up to you!' She held out her gift in her guilty hand, but Minos shrank back from what she offered him. Shaken at the thought of so unnatural a deed, he cried: 'You are a disgrace to our times! I pray that the gods may rid the earth of you, that land and sea may deny you any refuge! Certainly I shall not allow my world, the island of Crete which was the cradle of Jupiter, to come in contact with such a monster!' This was his reply. Then he imposed his own conditions, which were eminently just, upon his captured enemies and, when he had done so, ordered the mooring cables to be unloosed, and told the rowers to take their places in the bronze-beaked ships.

Scylla watched the ships being dragged down to

the sea and, when she saw them already afloat upon the waves, realized that the enemy leader was not going to reward her for her crime. She had no more prayers to utter; her mood changed to one of violent rage instead. In a fury, she tore her hair and shook her fists at Minos. 'Where are you going?' she cried. 'You whom I have preferred to my country and to my own father? Where are you going, leaving behind the one who made your recent conquest possible? Where are you off to, hard-hearted man, after gaining a victory for which I deserve all the credit and all the blame? Does the gift I have made you move you not at all? Does my love mean nothing, or the fact that all my hopes are centred on you alone? For, if you leave me, where shall I go? My own country lies vanquished and, even supposing it still survived, it is closed to me since I betrayed it. Shall I go to my father, after delivering him up to you? The citizens hate me, as they have every right to do, and neighbouring peoples are afraid of the example I have set. All the world is shut against me, so that Crete is my only refuge. If you prevent me from finding shelter there, if you are so lost to all sense of gratitude as to abandon me, then you are the son, not of Europa, but rather of the inhospitable Syrtis, of an Armenian tigress, or of Charybdis' pool, which the South wind lashes to fury: you are no child of Jove, and the story of your birth is a lie! It was not a god disguised as a bull who lured your mother away, but a real bull, a wild beast that had never known love for any heifer. O Nisus, my father, punish me! You walls that I lately betrayed, rejoice in my misfortunes! For I freely confess that I have earned your hatred, and that I deserve to die. But let it be one of those whom I have treacherously wronged who destroys me; why do you, Minos, punish my crime, when it has brought you victory? What my father and my country regard as guilt should be to you a proof of devotion. In very truth, that unfaithful wife who tricked a fierce bull by means of a wooden model, and bore a child half animal, half human, was a fit mate for you! Tell me, do my words reach your ears, or do those same winds that speed your ships carry away my pleas, you ungrateful wretch, and make them vain? Now, indeed, I am not surprised that Pasiphae preferred her bull to you: of the two, you were the more savage. Alas, he is ordering his crews to make haste: the wave roars under the beat of the oarblades, and I and my country together fade into the distance. But it is no use! You need not try to forget the service I have done you. I shall follow you, even against your will. I shall seize hold of your vessel's curving stern, and be carried with you far across the seas!'

No sooner had she said this, than she jumped into the water, and swam after the ships; her violent passion lending her strength, she grasped and clung to the Cretan vessel, an unwelcome companion. Her father caught sight of her (for he had been newly changed into a sea eagle, with tawny feathers, and was now hovering in the air) and attacked her, as she clung there, intending to rend her flesh with his hooked beak. In her terror she let go her hold on the boat, but as she fell the light breeze seemed to bear her up, and prevent her from touching the waters. She found herself all feathers: and when downy plumage had changed her into a bird she was called Ciris, or Shearer, a name she owes to the cutting off of her father's hair.

When Minos had returned safely to Crete, he disembarked, and sacrificed a hundred oxen to Jupiter in payment of his vows. The trophies he had won were hung up to adorn the palace. In his absence the monstrous child which the queen had borne, to the disgrace of the king's family, had grown up, and the strange hybrid creature had revealed his wife's disgusting love affair to everyone. Minos determined to rid his home of this shameful sight, by shutting the monster away in an enclosure of elaborate and involved design, where it could not be seen. Daedalus, an architect famous for his skill, constructed the maze, confusing the usual marks of direction, and leading the eye of the beholder astray by devious paths winding in different directions. Just as the playful waters of the Macander in Phrygia flow this way and that, without any consistency, as the river, turning to meet itself, sees its own advancing waves, flowing now towards its source and now towards the open sea, always changing its direction, so Daedalus constructed countless wandering paths and was himself scarcely able to find his way back to the entrance, so confusing was the maze.

There Minos imprisoned the monster, half-bull, half-man, and twice feasted him on Athenian blood; but when, after a further interval of nine years, a third band of victims was demanded, this brought about the creature's downfall. For, thanks to the help of the princess Ariadne, Theseus rewound the thread he had laid, retraced his steps, and found the elusive gateway as none of his predecessors had managed to do. Immediately he set sail for Dia, carrying with him the daughter of Minos; but on the shore of that island he cruelly abandoned his companion. Ariadne, left all alone, was sadly lamenting her fate, when Bacchus put his arms around her, and brought her his aid. He took the crown from her forehead and set it as a constellation in the sky, to bring her eternal glory. Up through the thin air it soared and, as it flew, its jewels were changed into shining fires. They settled in position, still keeping the appearance of a crown, midway between the kneeling Hercules and Ophiuchus, who grasps the snake.

Meanwhile Daedalus, tired of Crete and of his long absence from home, was filled with longing for his own country, but he was shut in by the sea. Then he said: 'The king may block my way by land or across the ocean, but the sky, surely, is open, and that is how we shall go. Minos may possess all the rest, but he does not possess the air.' With these words, he set his mind to sciences never explored before, and altered the laws of nature. He laid down a row of feathers, beginning with tiny ones, and gradually increasing their length, so that the edge seemed to slope upwards. In the same way, the pipe which shepherds used to play is built up from reeds, each slightly longer than the last. Then he fastened the feathers together in the middle with thread, and at the bottom with wax; when he had arranged them in this way, he bent them round into a gentle curve, to look like real birds' wings. His son Icarus stood beside him and, not knowing that the materials he was handling were to endanger his life, laughingly captured the feathers which blew away in the wind, or softened the yellow wax with his thumb, and by his pranks hindered the marvellous work on which his father was engaged.

When Daedalus had put the finishing touches to his invention, he raised himself into the air, balancing his body on his two wings, and there he hovered, moving his feathers up and down. Then he prepared his son to fly too. 'I warn you, Icarus,' he said, 'you must follow a course midway between earth and heaven, in case the sun should scorch your feathers, if you go too high, or the water make them heavy if you are too low. Fly halfway between the two. And pay no attention to the stars, to Bootes, or Helice or Orion with his drawn sword: take me as your guide, and follow me!'

While he was giving Icarus these instructions on how to fly, Daedalus was at the same time fastening the novel wings on his son's shoulders. As he worked and talked the old man's cheeks were wet with tears, and his fatherly affection made his hands tremble. He kissed his son, whom he was never to kiss again: then, raising himself on his wings, flew in front, showing anxious concern for his companion, just like a bird who has brought her tender fledgelings out of their nest in the tree-tops, and launched them into the air. He urged Icarus to follow close, and instructed him in the art that was to be his ruin, moving his own wings and keeping a watchful eye on those of his son behind him. Some fisher, perhaps, playing his quivering rod, some shepherd leaning on his staff, or a peasant bent over his plough handle caught sight of them as they flew past and stood stock still in astonishment, believing that these creatures who could fly through the air must be gods.

Now Juno's sacred isle of Samos lay on the left, Delos and Paros were already behind them, and

Lebinthus was on their right hand, along with Calymne, rich in honey, when the boy Icarus began to enjoy the thrill of swooping boldly through the air. Drawn on by his eagerness for the open sky, he left his guide and soared upwards, till he came too close to the blazing sun, and it softened the sweet-smelling wax that bound his wings together. The wax melted. Icarus moved his bare arms up and down, but without their feathers they had no purchase on the air. Even as his lips were crying his father's name, they were swallowed up in the deep blue waters which are called after him. The unhappy father, a father no longer, cried out: 'Icarus!' 'Icarus,' he called. 'Where are you? Where am I to look for you?' As he was still calling 'Icarus' he saw the feathers on the water, and cursed his inventive skill. He laid his son to rest in a tomb, and the land took its name from that of the boy who was buried there.

As Daedalus was burying the body of his ill-fated son, a chattering lapwing popped its head out of a muddy ditch, flapped its wings and crowed with joy. At that time it was the only bird of its kind, and none like it had ever seen before. The transformation had been a recent one, and was a lasting reproach to

Daedalus: for his sister, knowing nothing of fate's intention, had sent her son, an intelligent boy of twelve, to learn what Daedalus could teach him. This lad, observing the backbone of a fish, and taking it as a pattern, notched a series of teeth in a sharp iron blade, thus inventing the saw. He was the first, too, to fasten two iron arms together into one joint, so that, while remaining equidistant, one arm might stand still, and the other describe a circle round it. Daedalus was jealous, and flung his nephew headlong down from Minerva's sacred citadel. Then he spread a false report that the boy had fallen over. But Pallas, who looks favourably upon clever men, caught the lad as he fell and changed him into a bird, clothing him with feathers in mid-air. The swiftness of intellect he once displayed was replaced by swiftness of wing and foot. His name remained the same as before. However, this bird does not soar high into the air, nor does it build its nest on branches in the tree-tops: rather it flutters along the ground, and lays its eggs in the hedgerows, for it is afraid of heights, remembering its fall in the days of long ago.

Daedalus, weary with wandering, had now found refuge in Etna's land and Cocalus, who had taken up

arms in answer to his request for aid, had won a repu-
tation for clemency. Athens had now ceased to pay
her mournful tribute, thanks to Theseus' victory. The
temples were decked with garlands of flowers, and
the people were singing hymns to the warrior Min-
erva, to Jove, and to the other gods, honouring them
with gifts, with offerings of incense, and with the
sacrifices which they had promised. Rumour, swiftly
travelling, had spread Theseus' fame through the
various cities of Argos, and the peoples of rich Achaea
sought his help in their hour of peril. Among the rest,
Calydon begged and besought him to come to its
aid, though it had its own hero, Meleager. The request
was occasioned by a boar, which was at once the ser-
vant and the avenging minister of Diana. The goddess
was angry with the people: for, according to the tale,
King Oeneus, out of the bountiful harvests of a good
year, made offering of the first fruits of corn to Ceres,
poured a libation of wine in honour of Bacchus, and
one of olive oil in honour of Minerva. First the gods
of the farmers, and then all the gods in heaven,
received the honours they desired – except Leto's
daughter. She alone was neglected, and her altars
were the only ones left without an offering of incense.

Now the gods feel anger, too. 'I shall not submit to this without protest: men may say that I went unhonoured, but they will not say I went unavenged!' cried Diana; and she let loose a wild boar in Oeneus' land, to punish him for having scorned her. This boar was as big as the bulls found in grassy Epirus, bigger than the Sicilian ones. There was a fiery gleam in its bloodshot eyes, it held its neck high and stiff, its hide bristled with hairs that stuck straight out like spears. It bellowed harshly, the hot foam flecking its broad shoulders, and its teeth were like elephants' tusks: fire issued from its jaws, the leaves were set alight by its breath.

This monster trampled down the tender shoots of the growing crops, or again, when the harvest had fulfilled the farmers' hopes, it turned their joy to tears by ravaging the fields and breaking down the corn in the ear. The threshing floor and barns waited in vain for the promised harvests. Heavy vine clusters with their trailing leaves were strewn on the ground among berries and branches from the evergreen olive. The boar launched furious attacks on the flocks also: neither shepherds nor dogs could save them, nor could the fierce bulls defend the herds. People fled

in all directions, thinking themselves safe only when
protected by the walls of the city: till Meleager and
a handful of picked men banded themselves together
in a desire to win fame and glory.

There were the twin sons of Tyndareus, one
renowned as a boxer, and the other as a horseman:
Jason who had built the first ship, Theseus and Pir-
ithous, inseparable companions, and the two sons of
Thestius. Aphareus' sons were there, Lynceus and
swift Idas; Caeneus too, who had once been a woman,
the warrior Leucippus, Acastus, noted for his
javelin-throwing, Hippothous and Dryas, along with
Phoenix, Amyntor's son, the two sons of Actor, and
Phyleus who had come from Elis. Telamon joined
them, and Peleus, the father of great Achilles, as well
as the son of Pheres, and Iolaus from Boeotia. Eury-
tion was with them too, a man full of vigour, and
Echion, whom none could surpass in running, the
Locrian Lelex, and Panopeus and Hyleus, fierce Hip-
pasus and Nestor, then still in the prime of life. There
was also the contingent which Hippocoon had sent
from ancient Amyclae, and Penelope's father-in-law
Laertes came, accompanied by the Arcadian Ancaeus.
The wise seer, Ampycus' son, was there, and

Amphiaraus, who had not yet fallen a victim to his wife's treachery. The girl warrior from Tegea, the pride of the Lycaean grove, came too; a polished buckle fastened the neck of her garment, and her hair was simply done, gathered into a single knot. An ivory quiver, containing her arrows, hung from her left shoulder, and rattled as she moved, while she carried her bow as well, in her left hand. Such was her attire – she had features which in a boy would have been called girlish, but in a girl they were like a boy's.

As soon as the hero of Calydon saw her, he fell in love, though the gods would not sanction it, and was fired with secret desire. 'Happy indeed, the man whom she thinks worthy of her hand!' he sighed. He was too modest, and had no time, to say more; for there was a matter of greater urgency on hand, the mighty battle with the boar.

A dense forest of trees, which had never felt the woodman's axe, rose up from the level plain, affording a wide view over the sloping fields. When the warriors reached this wood, some of them spread out their hunting nets, some unleashed the dogs, while others, looking for danger, followed the trail of the boar's footprints. In the depths of a sunken hollow into which rainwater drained from above, grew pliant willows and thin sedge, marsh grasses and osiers and tall bullrushes, rising from a carpet of short reeds. The boar was driven out from this retreat, and rushed furiously into the midst of its foes, like a lightning flash struck out from the clouds as they are dashed together. Trees were brought down by its charge, and there was a sound of crashing as the animal blundered against their trunks. The young heroes raised a shout, and grasped their weapons in their strong hands, holding them poised for the throw, with broad iron tips thrust forward. The boar rushed on, scattering the dogs as they tried to block its furious onset, tossing the yapping beasts out of the way with side-long blows from its tusks. Echion hurled the first spear: but it missed its mark, and merely scarred the bark of a maple tree. The next missile looked as if it would lodge in the boar's back, but Jason of Pagasae, who threw it, put too much force behind the blow, and his spear overshot the mark. Then Mopsus, son of Ampycus, cried out: 'O Apollo, as I have worshipped you in the past, and do so still, grant that my spear may reach its mark: let there be no mistake!' The god granted his prophet's prayer as far as possible, for Mopsus struck the boar, but failed to wound it. As the weapon flew through the air, Diana had stolen away its iron tip, and only the wooden shaft, robbed of its point, reached its destination. But the boar's fury was roused, and blazed up as fiercely as the fire of a thunderbolt. Sparks flashed from its eyes, and it breathed out flames from its breast. Then, with unswerving attack, the murderous brute charged straight down on the band of young warriors, just as a massive rock, shot from the sling of a catapult, goes hurtling through the air towards enemy walls, or towers packed with soldiers. Eupalamus and Pelagon, who were keeping guard on the right, were flung to the ground, but their friends snatched them up from where they lay. Enaesimus, the son of Hippocoon, was not so lucky: he did not escape the boar's deadly tusks. Trembling with fear, he was preparing to run away, when the sinews behind his knees were slashed, and his muscles gave way beneath him. Nestor of Pylos, too, might well have perished before the time of the Trojan war, had he not used his spear as a vaulting pole, and leaped into the branches of a nearby tree, whence he looked down, from a safe

height, on the foe he had escaped. The boar fiercely
sharpened its tusks on the bark of an oak: then, con-
fident in its newly whetted weapons, returned to its
disastrous attacks, ripping open the thigh of the war-
rior Hippasus with its curved teeth. But now the twin
brothers, Castor and Pollux, not yet raised to be stars
in the heavens, rode up together, a striking pair on
their horses whiter than snow, and both together sent
their sharp javelins quivering through the air. They
would have wounded the bristling brute, had it not
retreated into the dark woods, where neither horse
nor javelin could penetrate. Telamon went after it
but, in his eagerness, he was careless of where he was
going, tripped over the root of a tree, and fell head-
long. While Peleus was helping him to his feet, the
girl from Tegea fitted an arrow to her bowstring: then,
bending the bow, she sent the shaft speeding through
the air. It grazed the top of the boar's back, and stuck
just below its ear, staining the bristles with a thin
trickle of blood. Meleager was as pleased at the girl's
success as she was herself. He was the first, so it is
thought, to see the blood and, having seen it, was
the first to point it out to his friends. 'You will be

honoured for your prowess as you deserve,' he told Atalanta.

The men flushed with shame, and urged each other on, shouting words of encouragement, and hurling their weapons without any concerted plan of attack. But just because they were so numerous, the missiles were rendered ineffective and prevented from reaching their mark. Then the Arcadian Ancaeus, armed with his two-headed axe, rushed furiously upon his fate, crying: 'See how far superior to a woman's weapons are those of a man! Make way for me! Even though Leto's daughter herself protect this boar with her own arrows, none the less, in spite of Diana, my hand will destroy it.' With these proud and boastful words, he raised his two-headed axe in both hands, and stood on tip-toe, bending forward, poised to strike. The boar charged down upon this daring foe and, aiming its tusks at the upper part of his loins, gored him in that most vital spot. Ancaeus collapsed: his inner organs slipped and trailed from his body in a mass of blood – the earth was soaked with the crimson stream. Pirithous, Ixion's son, rushed against the brute, brandishing his spears in his strong hand. But

Theseus, son of Aegeus, called to him: 'Heart of my heart, dearer than myself to me, stop at a safe distance! We can show our courage from afar: his hot-headed valour did Ancaeus no good!' As he spoke, he hurled his cornel spear with its heavy bronze tip: but though it was well thrown and would have reached its mark, it was stopped by the leafy branch of an oak. Jason, too, threw his javelin; but by bad luck his aim swerved, and the weapon killed an innocent hound, passing through its thighs, and pinning it to the ground. Meleager, son of Oeneus, threw two spears, with very different effect: for the first stuck in the ground, but the other lodged right in the middle of the boar's back. Without loss of time, while the beast was furiously twisting its body round and round, its jaws slavering with a mixture of foam and fresh blood, the hero who had dealt the wound came up close to the animal, and roused his foe to fury, before finally burying his shining spear in its shoulder. His friends cheered with delight, and made a rush to shake the victor by the hand. They gazed with wonder at the huge beast that covered so much ground as it lay and, convinced that it was still unsafe to go near, each one of them stained his own weapon in the blood of the boar.

Meleager himself set his foot on its monstrous head: then, turning to Atalanta, 'Take the spoil I have secured, lady of Nonacris,' he said, 'and let me share my glory with you.' Thereupon he gave her as a trophy the bristling hide, and the boar's head, with its magnificent tusks. She was as pleased with the giver of the gift as with the gift itself: but the others were jealous, and a murmur ran through the whole company. Then the two sons of Thestius shook their fists and shouted: 'Come now, put down these spoils, woman, and do not interfere with our claims to honour! Do not let confidence in your beauty mislead you, either, in case your love-sick benefactor should prove unable to help you.' Then they took away the spoils from Atalanta, and deprived Meleager of the right to present them to her. The son of Mars could not endure this; bursting with rage, gnashing his teeth, he cried: 'You robbers, stealing another man's glory! I shall teach you the difference between threats and action!' and he ran his sword through the heart of Plexippus who was standing by, all unsuspecting.

It was an abominable deed. Toxeus hesitated as to what he should do, for he wished to avenge his brother, but at the same time was afraid of sharing his fate: Meleager did not suffer him to hesitate for long, for he plunged his weapon, still reeking with the murder of one brother, into the warm blood of the other.

Althaea had been told of her son's victory, and was already carrying offerings to the temple of the gods, when she saw her brothers being brought home dead. The city was filled with her wailing, as she gave vent to her clamorous grief: she beat her breast, and changed the gold-embroidered robes she wore for black clothing. However, when she heard who had killed her brothers, she forgot her grief, and turned from tears to concentrate on revenge.

There was a log, which the three sister goddesses had placed on the fire, at the time when this Althaea, Thestius' daughter, was lying in bed with her baby newly born. As they spun the threads of destiny, holding them firmly under their thumbs, they said: 'To the log and to the new-born child we assign the same span of years.' As soon as the goddesses had recited their verses and left the house, the mother snatched the blazing log from the fire, and flung cold water on it. For long it had been hidden away in the depths of the house, and its preservation had kept the young hero safe too. Now his mother brought it out, called for chips of pine wood and shavings, and when these had been piled up, kindled the flames that were to be her son's undoing. Then four times she tried to throw the log on the flames, and four times she stopped herself. Her affection for her son fought against her feelings for her brothers, and divided loyalty tore her heart in opposite directions. Often her face grew pale with fear at the thought of such a crime, often blazing anger made her eyes sparkle with fire. At times her expression was cruel and threatening, at others it could have been thought to be full of compassion. The heat of her fierce rage dried up her tears, yet still the tears welled up, and like a ship which feels the double pull as wind and tides draw it in different directions, as it sways uncertainly with both, so Thestius' daughter was swayed by her shifting emotions, and her anger alternately died away and flared up again. However, her sisterly affection began to get the better of her feelings as a mother, and in order to satisfy her brothers' ghosts with blood, by a guilty deed she saved herself from guilt. When the deadly flames were burning steadily: 'Let this funeral pyre consume the child I bore!' she cried. Then, taking the fateful log in her murderous hands, the wretched woman stood before the funeral altars and prayed: 'Goddesses three, who preside over punishments, Furies, behold this unnatural sacrifice, by which I am at once avenging and committing crime. Death must atone for death, wickedness be piled on wickedness, slaughter upon slaughter, till this accursed household perish under its accumulation of woe. Shall Oeneus continue to enjoy the company of his victorious son, while Thestius is deprived of his? Better that both should have cause to mourn! Only do you, my brothers, ghosts but recently descended to the shades, recognize my devotion, and welcome this offering provided at such a cost, the child of my womb, born to my sorrow!

'Alas, where do I rush so fast? O my brothers, forgive a mother! My hands cannot carry out their purpose: I confess my son has deserved to die, but I cannot bear that I should be the author of his death. Will he then go unpunished? Will he live, a victorious hero, exulting in this very exploit, ruling the kingdom of Calydon, while you lie dead, nothing but chill ghosts and a few ashes? No, that I cannot endure. Let the guilty wretch perish too, and carry with him to the grave his father's hopes, his kingdom, and his ruined country. But where is the affection a mother should feel for her son? Where are the loving ties that ought to bind parents to their children. Where the anguish I endured through ten long months? O my son, how much better had I allowed you to burn in those flames, when you were a baby! You received your life from my hands, but now you will die the death you have deserved! Accept the reward for what you have done: give me back the life I have twice bestowed on you, once when you were born, and again when I snatched the log from the fire. Either that, or send me to join my brothers in the tomb!

'I want to, yet I cannot! What am I to do? At one moment I see before my eyes my brothers' wounds, and a vision of their dreadful murder: the next, my love for my son, the name of mother, break my resolution. Poor wretch that I am! It will be an evil thing, my brothers, if you triumph – yet triumph, none the less, provided that I too may follow you to the shades, you and the son I sacrifice to solace you!' With these words she flung the fatal log, with unsteady hands, into the heart of the flames, turning her face away as she did so. The very wood groaned, or seemed to groan, as it was kindled and set alight by the unwilling fire.

Meleager, though he knew nothing of what was happening, and was not even present, was scorched by that flame, and felt a hidden fire consuming his vitals. He endured his agony with indomitable courage; but still, he grieved that he should meet so inglorious an end, that his death involved no bloodshed, and declared Ancaeus lucky to have suffered the wounds he did. For the last time he called upon his aged father, his brothers and loving sisters, cried out his wife's name, groaning as he did so, and perhaps his mother's too. As the fire blazed up, so did his agony: then both died down again, and were extinguished together. Gradually his breath dispersed into the thin air, as the white ash gradually settled over the glowing embers.

The highlands of Calydon were prostrate with grief. Young men and old were in mourning, the common people and the leaders of the country all lamented. The women who dwelt by Evenus' stream tore their hair and beat their breasts. Meleager's father lay prone upon the ground, his white hair and age-worn face begrimed with dust, complaining bitterly that he had lived too long. As for his mother, knowing full well the dreadful thing she had done, with her own guilty hand she exacted punishment from herself, driving a sword through her own body.

Though the gods had given me a hundred mouths and a hundred tongues, poetic genius and all Helicon for my province, still I could not adequately express the sad laments of Meleager's unhappy sisters. Heedless of what was seemly, they beat their bruised breasts and, while their brother's body remained, fondled and cherished it, kissing the poor corpse, and the bier on which it lay. When his limbs had been reduced to ashes, they gathered these together, and clasped them to their breasts: then they flung themselves on the ground by his grave and, embracing the tombstone, bathed the name inscribed there with their tears. At last Diana was content with the disasters which had befallen the house of Parthaon; she raised the girls into the air, all except Gorge and great Alcmene's daughter-in-law, causing feathers to sprout from their bodies, and stretching wings along their arms. She gave them horny beaks and, when she had so changed them, dispatched them into the sky.

Meanwhile Theseus, having played his part in the joint enterprise, was making his way back to Athena's city where Erechtheus once ruled, when Achelous, swollen with rain, blocked his path, and forced him to delay. 'Come into my house, great Athenian,' said the river god, 'and do not trust yourself to my greedy flood. These waters, as they roar in their slanting channel, are wont to sweep away massive tree trunks, and hurl rocks along. I have seen great stables, cattle and all, swept from their sites upon my banks: and then the oxen could make no use of their sturdy strength, nor could the horses use their speed. Many a young man, too, has been drowned in these turbulent waters, when melting snows from the mountains have swollen my torrent. It is safer to wait quietly, till my river runs within its usual limits and, reduced to a slender stream, is contained in its own channel.' Aegeus' son agreed with the river, and replied: 'I shall take your advice, Achelous, and seek shelter in your home.' He did as he said, and entered the caves built of porous pumice and rough tufa stone. The ground was damp with soft moss, the ceiling roofed with alternate bands of conch shells and shells of purple fish.

Now the sun had travelled two thirds of the way across the sky, when Theseus and his companions took their places on the couches. On one side of Theseus was the son of Ixion, on the other the hero Lelex from Troezen, whose hair was already streaked with white at the temples. Others too, were there, whom the Acarnanian river god had deemed worthy of sharing the honour of Theseus' company, for Achelous was highly delighted to have so distinguished a guest. The nymphs, bare-footed, at once set out the tables and loaded them with good things: afterwards, when the banquet had been cleared away, they served wine in jewelled cups. Then Theseus, bravest of heroes, looked out over the waters that stretched before his eyes, and pointing with his finger, said: 'Tell me, what place is that? What is the name of that island? Though it looks like more than one.' 'What you see is not one island,' answered the river. 'There are five there, but the distance prevents your seeing that they are separate. Do not be too astonished at what Diana did to Calydon when she was scorned: for these used to be naiads! But on one occasion, after they had made a sacrifice of ten bullocks, they invited all the other rural deities to their festival, and proceeded with their festival dances, quite forgetting me! I swelled with rage, till my waters were as full as they are when at their fullest. Then, with heart and flood equally ruthless, I tore apart forest from forest, field from field, and in my swirling tide swept down to the sea the nymphs and their dancing floor. Then, at last, too late, did they remember me. My waves and those of the ocean split that piece of land apart and divided it into as many portions as you see islands, dotted over the ocean. They are called the Echinades. But there is one, look, which you see for yourself lies far apart from the others, and it is dear to me. The sailors call it Perimele. I fell in love with that girl, and robbed her of her maidenhood, a thing which outraged her father Hippodamas so much that he hurled his daughter from a cliff into the sea, intending to kill her. But I caught her up, and sup-ported her as she swam. As I did so, I prayed to Neptune: "You to whose lot has fallen the kingdom of the restless sea, next in importance to that of heaven, lend us your aid, great god of the trident, and grant a place, I pray you, to one drowned by her

father's cruelty: or else let her become herself a place."
While I was still speaking land, newly formed,
embraced her floating limbs, and a massive island
materialized on top of her changed body.'

His story finished, the river god fell silent. The
whole company was stirred by the miracle he had
related, but Ixion's son laughed at them for believing
the tale. Arrogant and contemptuous of the gods as
he was, he challenged his host. 'Your story is pure
invention, Achelous,' he said. 'You put too much
faith in the power of the gods, if you think they can
give and take away the shapes of things.' All were
dumbfounded, and disapproved of such words, but
before anyone else could speak Lelex, ripe in years
and wisdom, broke in: 'The power of heaven is meas-
ureless, and knows no bounds; whatever the gods
wish is at once achieved. Here is a story which will
convince you.

'In the hill-country of Phrygia there is an oak,
growing close beside a linden tree, and a low wall
surrounds them both. I have seen the spot myself,
for Pittheus sent me on a mission to that land, where
his father Pelops once was king. Not far off is a stag-
nant pool: once it was habitable country, but now it

has become a stretch of water, haunted by marsh birds, divers and coots. Jupiter visited this place, disguised as a mortal, and Mercury, the god who carries the magic wand, laid aside his wings and accompanied his father. The two gods went to a thousand homes, looking for somewhere to rest, and found a thousand homes bolted and barred against them. However, one house took them in: it was, indeed, a humble dwelling roofed with thatch and reeds from the marsh, but a good-hearted old woman, Baucis by name, and her husband Philemon, who was the same age as his wife, had been married in that cottage in their youth, and had grown grey in it together. By confessing their poverty and accepting it contentedly, they had eased the hardship of their lot. It made no difference in that house whether you asked for master or servant – the two of them were the entire household: the same people gave the orders and carried them out. So, when the heaven-dwellers reached this humble home and, stooping down, entered its low doorway, the old man set chairs for them, and invited them to rest their weary limbs; Baucis bustled up anxiously to throw a rough piece of cloth over the chairs, and stirred up the warm ashes on the hearth, fanning the remains of yesterday's fire, feeding it with leaves and chips of dried bark, and blowing on it till it burst into flames. Then the old woman took down finely split sticks and dry twigs which were hanging from the roof, broke them into small pieces, and pushed them under her little pot. Her husband had brought in some vegetables from his carefully watered garden, and these she stripped of their outer leaves. Philemon took a two-pronged fork and lifted down a side of smoked bacon that was hanging from the blackened rafters; then he cut off a small piece of their long-cherished meat, and boiled it till it was tender in the bubbling water. Meanwhile the old couple chattered on, to pass the time, and kept their guests from noticing the delay. There was a beech-wood bowl there, hanging from a nail by its curved handle, which was filled with warm water, and the visitors washed in this, to refresh themselves. On a couch with frame and legs of willow-wood lay a mattress, stuffed with soft sedge grass. Baucis and Philemon covered this with the cloths which they used to put out only on solemn holidays – even so, the stuff was old and cheap, a good match for the willow couch. Then the gods took their places for the

37

meal. Old Baucis tucked up her dress and, with shaky hands, set the table down in front of them. One of its three legs was shorter than the others, but she pushed a tile in below, to make it the same height. When she had inserted this, and so levelled the sloping surface, she wiped over the table with some stalks of fresh mint. Then she placed upon the board the mottled berry which honest Minerva loves, wild cherries picked in the autumn and preserved in lees of wine, endives and radishes and a piece of cheese, and eggs lightly roasted in ashes not too hot; all these were set out in clay dishes and, after they had been served, a flagon with a raised pattern, just as much silver as their dinner service, was set on the table, and beech-wood cups, lined inside with yellow wax. After a short while, the hearth provided them with food piping hot and the wine, which was of no great age, was sent round again. Then it was set aside for a little, to make way for dessert, which consisted of nuts, a mixture of figs and wrinkled dates, plums and fragrant apples in shallow baskets, and black grapes, just gathered. A shining honey-comb was set in the midst of these good things and, above all, there was cheerful company, and bustling hospitality, far beyond their means.

'As the dinner went on, the old man and woman saw that the flagon, as often as it was emptied, refilled itself of its own accord, and that the wine was automatically replenished. At the sight of this miracle, Baucis and Philemon were awed and afraid. Timidly stretching out their hands in prayer, they begged the gods' indulgence for a poor meal, without any elaborate preparations. They had a single goose, which acted as guardian of their little croft: in honour of their divine visitors, they were making ready to kill the bird, but with the help of its swift wings it eluded its owners for a long time, and tired them out, for age made them slow. At last it seemed to take refuge with the gods themselves, who declared that it should not be killed. 'We are gods,' they said, 'and this wicked neighbourhood is going to be punished as it richly deserves; but you will be allowed to escape this disaster. All you have to do is to leave your home, and climb up the steep mountainside with us.' The two old people both did as they were told and, leaning on their sticks, struggled up the long slope.

'When they were a bowshot distant from the top, they looked round and saw all the rest of their country drowned in marshy waters, only their own home left standing. As they gazed in astonishment, and wept for the fate of their people, their old cottage, which had been small, even for two, was changed into a temple: marble columns took the place of its wooden supports, the thatch grew yellow, till the roof seemed to be made of gold, the doors appeared magnificently adorned with carvings, and marble paved the earthen floor. Then Saturn's son spoke in majestic tones: "Tell me, my good old man, and you, who are a worthy wife for your good husband, what would you like from me?' Philemon and Baucis consulted together for a little, and then the old man told the gods what they both wished. 'We ask to be your priests, to serve your shrine; and since we have lived in happy companionship all our lives, we pray that death may carry us off together at the same instant, so that I may never see my wife's funeral, and she may never have to bury me.' Their prayer was granted. They looked after the temple as long as they lived.

'Then, one day, bowed down with their weight of years, they were standing before the sacred steps, talking of all that had happened there, when Baucis saw Philemon beginning to put forth leaves, and old Philemon saw Baucis growing leafy too. When the tree-tops were already growing over their two faces, they exchanged their last words while they could, and cried simultaneously: "Good-bye, my dear one!" As they spoke, the bark grew over and concealed their lips. The Bithynian peasant still points out the trees growing there side by side, trees that were once two bodies. This tale was told me by responsible old men, who had nothing to gain by deceiving me. Indeed, I myself have seen the wreaths hanging on the branches, and have hung up fresh ones, saying: "Whom the gods love are gods themselves, and those who have worshipped should be worshipped too."'

That was the end of his story. Both the story-teller and the tale he told excited the whole company, but Theseus most of all. As he was clamouring to hear more of the wonderful deeds of the gods, the river god of Calydon raised himself on his elbow, and addressed the hero in these words: 'There are some, bravest Theseus, whose shape has been changed just once, and has then remained permanently altered. Others again have power to change into several forms. Take, for instance, Proteus, the god who dwells in the sea that encircles the earth. People have seen him at one time in the shape of a young man, at another transformed into a lion; sometimes he used to appear to them as a raging wild boar, or again as a snake, which they shrank from touching; or else horns transformed him into a bull. Often he could be seen as a stone, or a tree, sometimes he presented the appearance of running water, and became a river, sometimes he was the very opposite, when he turned into fire.

'The wife of Autolycus, who was Erysichthon's daughter, had the same power. Her father was a man who scorned the gods, and never made any offering of incense on the altars. He is even reported to have used his sacrilegious axe on the trees of Ceres' grove, violating the ancient woodlands with its blade. Among these trees there stood a huge oak, which had grown sturdy and strong in the course of years, a forest in itself, hung round with wreaths and garlands and votive tablets, tributes for prayers that had been granted. Under this tree the dryads often held their festive dances, often they joined hands in a circle and embraced its trunk, whose circumference measured fifteen cubits. In height, too, it towered above the other trees, as much as they did above the grassy sward. Yet this did not deter Erysichthon from wielding his axe against it. He ordered his servants to cut down the sacred tree and, when he saw them hesitate to carry out his commands, the scoundrel snatched an axe from one of the men, and shouted: 'Should this tree be itself a goddess, and not just a tree the goddess loves, still its leafy top will be brought down to earth!' As he uttered these words, he held his weapon poised, ready to strike the trunk obliquely. The oak tree of Ceres trembled and groaned: at the same time, the leaves and acorns began to turn white, and the long branches lost their colour. Then, when his impious hand had made a gash in its trunk, blood flowed out where the bark was split open, just as it pours from the severed neck of some mighty bull, slain before the altars as an offering. Everyone stood still in horrified amazement: out of all the company, one man dared to try to prevent the sacrilege, to stop the cruel axe. Thessalian Erysichthon glared at him: 'Take that as a reward for your pious thoughts!' he stormed, and swung his axe against the man instead of the tree, lopping off his head. Then he turned again to the oak, and dealt it blow after blow.

43

'Meanwhile, from the heart of the tree, a voice was heard saying: "I who dwell within this tree am a nymph, whom Ceres dearly loves. I warn you with my dying breath, that punishment for your wickedness is at hand: that thought comforts me in death." But Erysichthon persisted in his criminal action. When the tree had at length been weakened by innumerable blows, ropes were attached to the trunk, and it was brought crashing down, creating havoc in the wood as it fell, by reason of its great weight. All her sister dryads, sorely distressed at the loss which the grove and they themselves had suffered, dressed themselves in black garments, and mournfully approached Ceres, begging that Erysichthon should be punished. That most beautiful goddess consented; nodding her head, she made the fields, laden with heavy harvests, tremble, as she devised a punishment which would have made its victim an object of pity indeed, if he had not forfeited all men's pity by his deeds. She planned to torment him with deadly Hunger.

'Since destiny does not allow Ceres and Hunger to meet, she could not approach this creature herself, but she gave orders to a rustic oread, one of the mountain spirits. "There is a place," she said, "which lies far off, in the icy land of Scythia, a gloomy barren spot where the earth knows nothing of crops or trees. It is the home of sluggish Chill, of Pallor and Ague, and ravening Hunger lives there too. Go, then, bid Hunger bury herself in the wicked stomach of this impious wretch: tell her to fight and overcome my powers of nourishment, and to let no amount of food defeat her. Do not be frightened at the length of the journey; take my chariot and my dragons and drive them through the air." Ceres then handed over her car, and the oread was borne through the skies in the borrowed chariot.

'She alighted in Scythia, and there unyoked her dragons on the summit of a rocky mountain, which the inhabitants call Caucasus. She went to look for Hunger, whom she found in a stony field, tearing up a few scant grasses with her nails and her teeth. The creature's face was colourless, hollow-eyed, her hair uncared for, her lips bleached and cracked. Scabrous sores encrusted her throat, her skin was hard and transparent, revealing her inner organs. The brittle bones stuck out beneath her hollow loins, and instead of a stomach she had only a place for one. Her breast, hanging loose, looked as if it were held in position only by the framework of her spine. Her joints seemed large in contrast to her skinny limbs, the curve of her knees made a real swelling, and her ankle-bones formed protuberances that were out of all proportion. When the oread saw her, she did not venture to go up close, but delivered the goddess's orders from a distance and, in a very short time, though she had only just come, and though she remained a good way off, she seemed herself to feel the pangs of hunger. Turning her team, she drove the dragons back through the air to Haemonia.

'Although she is always opposed to Ceres' activities, Hunger obeyed the goddess's instructions. The wind carried her through the air till she came to the house she had been told to visit. Immediately she entered the bedroom of the scoundrel Erysichthon. Finding him sound asleep (for it was night-time) she flung both her arms around him, insinuated herself into her victim, breathing into his lips, his throat, his heart, and spread famishing hunger through his hollow veins. When she had carried out her orders, she left the fertile world again, and returned to her poverty-stricken home and her accustomed haunts.

'Erysichthon was still slumbering peacefully, soothed by the wings of the gentle god of sleep, but he dreamed that he was feasting, and chewed uselessly at nothing, grinding his teeth together, and cheating himself by swallowing a mere pretence of food. Instead of a banquet he gulped down insubstantial air, all to no purpose. When he awoke, he was furiously hungry: his famished jaws and burning stomach were utterly at the mercy of his craving. Without delay, he gave orders for all the foodstuffs that earth and air and sea provide to be brought to him, complained of hunger when the laden tables were set before him, and in the midst of feasting sought still more feasts. Supplies which would have satisfied whole cities or an entire nation were not enough for him, and the more he ate, the more he desired. As the sea receives rivers from all over the earth and yet has always room for more, and drinks up the waters from distant lands, or as greedy flames never refuse nourishment, but burn up countless faggots, made hungrier by the very abundance of supplies and requiring more, the more they are given: so the jaws of the scoundrel Erysichthon welcomed all the provisions that were offered, and at the same time asked for more. All the food he consumed only excited his desire for food, and by eating he continually produced an aching void.

'Now, thanks to this hunger, to the bottomless pit that was his stomach, his family fortunes had dwindled away: but still his dreadful hunger remained, not diminished in the slightest. His burning appetite was unabated. At length, when he had eaten up all his wealth, he was left with only his daughter, a girl who deserved to have had a better parent. In his penniless state, he sold her too: but she was a girl of spirit, and rebelled against having a master. Stretching out her hands over the nearby waters, she cried: "You who robbed me of my maidenhood, and have your reward, rescue me from slavery!" Neptune was the one who had the reward of which she spoke, and he did not scorn her prayer. Although her owner, coming along behind, had seen the girl only a moment before, the god changed her shape, gave her the face of a man, and dressed her in fisherman's clothes. Her master came up and, looking straight at her, said: "You there, concealing your dangling hooks with tiny bits of bait, you with the rod in your hands, I wish you a calm sea, and gullible fishes that never notice the hook till they are caught, if you will tell me where the girl is, who was standing on the shore just now, with her hair all disordered, dressed in cheap clothes. I saw her on the sands: but tell me, where is she? For her footprints go no further."

'The other, realizing that what the god had done for her had been successful, was delighted that she herself should be asked where she was. In reply to her master's question, she said: "Excuse me, whoever you are. I have never taken my eyes off this pool, and have been entirely occupied with my fishing. To remove any doubts you may have, I swear, so may the god of the sea assist me in my livelihood, that no one but myself has been on this shore for a long time, and no woman has set foot here." The man believed her and, turning round, walked away over the sand, cheated of his slave. Then the girl's true shape was restored to her.

'Her father, when he perceived that his daughter could undergo such transformations, often sold her to different masters, and she escaped in the form of a horse, or a bird, or again as an ox or a stag, thus obtaining provisions, dishonestly, for her gluttonous father. However, when in the violence of his malady he had consumed all that was offered and had thus merely aggravated his grievous sickness, the wretch began to bite and gnaw at his own limbs, and fed his body by eating it away.

'But why do I waste time over tales of other people? I myself, my young friend, have the power to alter my body, though the number of shapes I can assume is limited. Sometimes I appear as you see me now, sometimes I change into a snake, or again I become a bull, the leader of the herd, whose strength lies in his horns – horns, I say, for I had two while I could. But now, as you see for yourself, one side of my forehead has lost its weapon' . . . and his words gave place to groans.

Then Neptune's son, brave Theseus, asked Achelous why he was groaning, and how his forehead had come by this injury. The river of Calydon, who wore a circlet of reeds on his tangled locks, answered him in these words: 'It is a painful thing you ask of me: who would want to speak of battles in which he had been defeated? However, I shall tell you what happened: for the glory of having fought is greater than the disgrace of having been beaten, and I am much consoled in my defeat by the thought that my opponent was so great a hero.

'Perhaps you have heard tell of Deianira? She was a most lovely girl who, in days gone by, roused jealous hopes in the hearts of many suitors and I, along with the rest, went to the house of the man I hoped would be my father-in-law. "Son of Parthaon," I said, "take me as your daughter's husband." My words were echoed by Hercules, whereupon the other suitors left the field to us two. My rival declared that he would give his bride Jupiter as a father-in-law, and called to mind his own famous Labours, and the fact that he had succeeded in carrying out his stepmother's commands. I countered his claims, saying: "It is disgraceful that a god should yield place to mortal." – for in those days Hercules was not yet a god – "In me you see the king of the waters which flow through your country in their slanting channels. As a son-in-law I shall not be a stranger, sent from foreign shores, but one of your own people, and a part of your kingdom. Only do not hold it against me that Juno, queen of heaven, does not hate me, that I have never been punished by having labours imposed upon me!

'"As to your other point, son of Alcmene, Jupiter whom you boastfully declare to be your father, is either not your father at all, or if he is, it was guilt that made him so! When you claim him as father, you convict your mother of adultery. Choose whether you prefer to say that Jove is not really your father, or to admit that you were born as a result of a piece of disgraceful behaviour."

'Hercules had long been glowering at me as I spoke. Instead of controlling his flaring rage, as a hero should, he retorted: "I am better with my hands than with my tongue: provided I can defeat you in the fight, you can have your verbal victory!" and he rushed fiercely upon me. I was ashamed to draw back, after my recent boasting. Flinging off my garments, I raised my arms, held them crooked before my chest in a position of defence, and prepared myself to fight. My opponent sprinkled me with dust that he had gathered in his cupped palms, and in his turn was covered with yellow sand, till he was all golden. Then he clutched at my neck, and again at my rapidly shifting legs, or seemed to clutch, attacking me from every angle. But my weight was my salvation. I was impervious to his assaults, just as a massive rock, besieged by the roaring waves, stands fast and is kept safe by its very bulk.

'We drew a little apart, and then rushed to join battle again, each holding his ground, determined not to yield, foot pressed against foot. Leaning forward from the waist, I thrust my fingers against his fingers, my head against his head. I have seen sturdy bulls rush upon one another, in just the same way, when they are fighting to win the sleekest cow in all the meadows for their prize. The herds look on, trembling, not knowing which will be the victor, and gain such mastery. Three times Hercules tried, without avail, to thrust away my breast that was locked against his own; at the fourth attempt he shook off my grip, and loosened my straining arms. Then, striking me a blow that whirled me about (for I am resolved to tell the truth), he flung himself, with all his weight, upon my back, and clung there. Believe me, I am not just trying to enhance your respect for me – it is no exaggeration to say that I really seemed to be crushed down by a mountain on top of me. However, I barely managed to insert my arms, streaming with sweat, beneath his body, and so with difficulty was able to loosen his cruel grip on my breast. Still he pressed me hard, and prevented me, panting and breathless as I was, from recovering my strength. In this way he got control of my neck and then, at last, I was forced to my knees, and bit the dust.

'Proved inferior to him in valour, I had resort to stratagems, and slipped from the hero's grasp by turning myself into a long snake. But when I had coiled my body into sinuous spirals, and was flickering my forked tongue, hissing fiercely, Hercules of Tiryns laughed, and mocked my tricks. "I was defeating snakes in my cradle!" he cried, "and though you may be more terrible than any other, Achelous, yet you are only one solitary serpent, and how small a part of the Lernaean hydra that will be! The hydra throve on its wounds, and none of its hundred heads could be cut off with impunity, without being replaced by two new ones which made its neck stronger than ever. Yet, in spite of its branching snakes, reborn as they were cut down, in spite of the strength it derived from attempts to harm it, still I got the upper hand of the hydra, vanquished the monster, and ripped its body open. Imagine, then, what will happen to you, who have changed yourself into a mere semblance of a snake, employing weapons that are not natural to you, and concealing yourself under a borrowed shape!" With these words, he fastened his fingers tightly round the upper part of my throat. I was being throttled, as if my neck were caught in a vice, and struggled to wrest my jaws out of the grip of his thumbs.

'So he overcame me in this guise too; but there remained my third shape, that of a fierce bull. I therefore transformed myself into a bull, and as such renewed the fight. My adversary, attacking from the left, flung his arms round the bulging muscles of my neck. As I charged away, he followed close beside me, dragging at my head, till he forced my horns into the hard ground, and laid me prostrate in the deep dust. Nor was this enough: as he grasped my stiff horn in his cruel hand, he broke and tore it off, mutilating my brow. But the naiads filled it with fruits and fragrant flowers, and sanctified it, and now my horn enriches the Goddess of Plenty.' When he had finished speaking, one of his attendants, a nymph dressed in the style of Diana, came forward, her hair streaming over her shoulders, and brought all autumn's harvest in the rich horn, with delicious apples for their dessert.

Dawn came, and when the first rays of the sun struck the mountaintops, the young men went on their way; for they did not wait till the river was flowing peacefully and smoothly, nor even till all the floods had subsided. Achelous hid his rustic features and the head that had lost its horn in the depths of his waters.